Sing, Clap and Play the Recorder

Book 1

A descant recorder book for beginners

By Heather Cox and Garth Rickard

Original design and illustrations by David Woodroffe

Revised design and layout by Camden Music

Published by

EJA Publications

14-15 Berners Street, London W1T 3LJ, UK

Exclusive Distributors:

Music Sales Limited

Newmarket Road, Bury St. Edmunds, Suffolk IP33 3YB, UK

Music Sales Pty Limited

20 Resolution Drive, Caringbah, NSW 2229, Australia

Music Sales Corporation

257 Park Avenue South, New York, NY 10010, USA

To the teacher

School music is often considered a special subject which must be taught by experts. This can leave pupils with no music or waiting for a once-a-week lesson with a specialist. *Sing, Clap and Play*, however, is written specifically to enable the teacher with little or no musical background to teach the recorder easily and with confidence, and practical hints for teachers are printed in boxes throughout the book. Specialist teachers may also find it a useful backbone for their course.

The learning is divided into three stages, and a 'concert' is included at the end of every stage which provides a set of performance pieces. These enable pupils to feel a sense of achievement and celebrate their progress. A CD edition of this book is available, containing backing tracks and demonstration performances of all concert pieces. Much of the *Sing, Clap and Play* material could also be performed, making concerts a way of life.

We suggest one half-hour session per week, and five minutes every day for practice—the book will then take approximately two terms to complete.

The sequence 'sing, clap and play' is fundamental since singing and clapping helps the child establish the rhythm through the words, and in time begin to associate a pitch with a written note. The book is aimed at 7 to 11 year-olds (Key Stage 2).

Introduction

This is your recorder.

Hold it between the fingers and thumb of your **left** hand.

Support it with the thumb of your **right** hand.

Until you are ready to play, rest the mouthpiece
on your chin.*

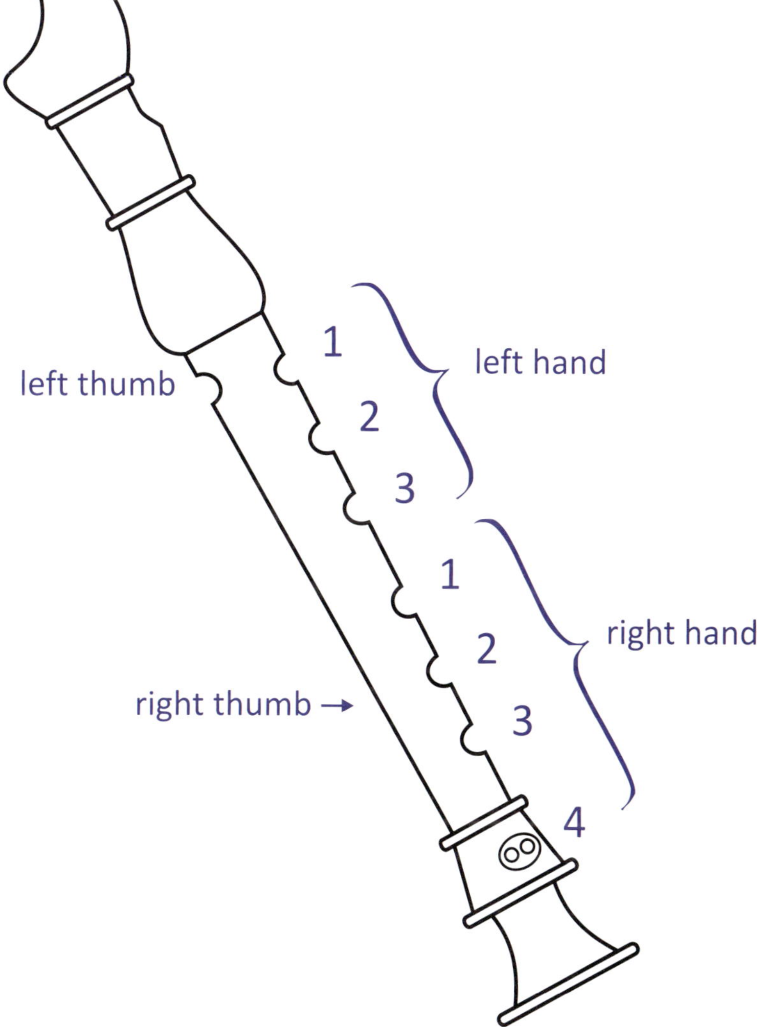

* This is always useful while practising fingering
as it avoids unwanted notes.

Lesson 1

To play the note *B*, lift up all your fingers, except the first finger of your left hand and your left thumb.*

Place your lips over the mouthpiece and make your tongue say 'doo' into the recorder.**

Try this several times, blowing softly and making all the notes sound the same.***

* Fingers not in use should be kept close to the holes so that they will be ready when needed.

** Every note at this stage should be tongued to give a clear beginning.

*** For a well-pitched note, blowing softly is essential.

B

Sing, Clap and Play 1

Here is your first song.

1. Sing it
2. Clap it
3. Play it*

Practise this several times, and then go on to the other songs.

Boots!

Count **:

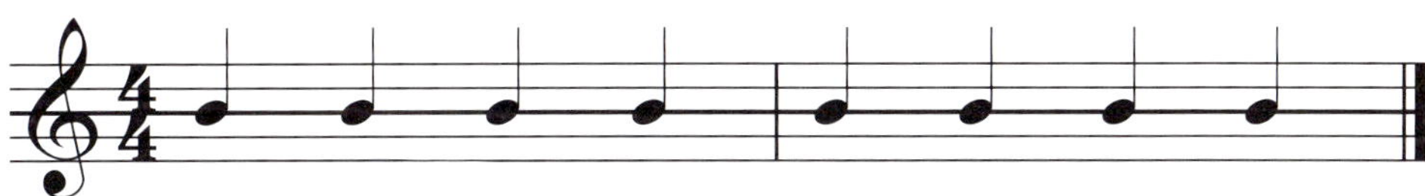

Bach

Count:

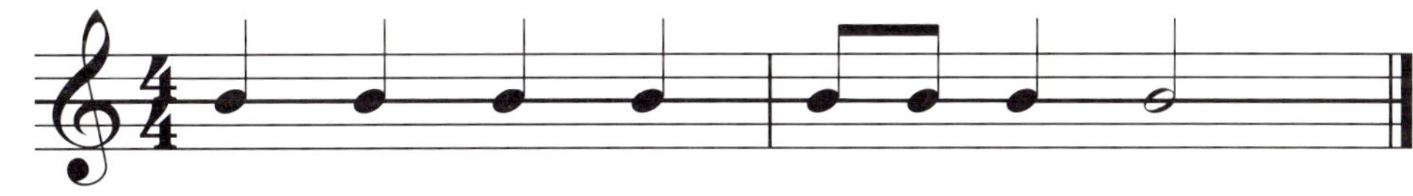

* It is important in every song to sing and clap before playing to ensure the rhythm is correct.

** A steady count will indicate the speed of the song, and will start everyone together.

Big, bad Bill

Count:

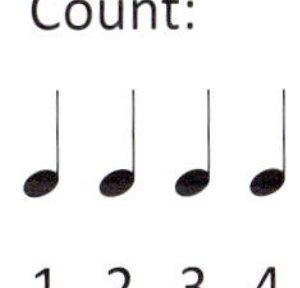

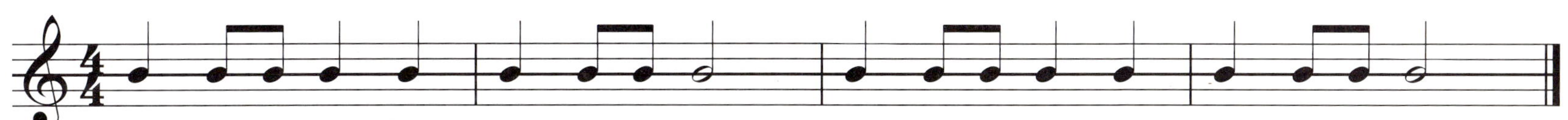

Lesson 2

The note *A* is played with the first two fingers and thumb of your *left* hand.*

Keep your other fingers close to the holes.

Practise *A* several times, and then go on to SING, CLAP and PLAY.

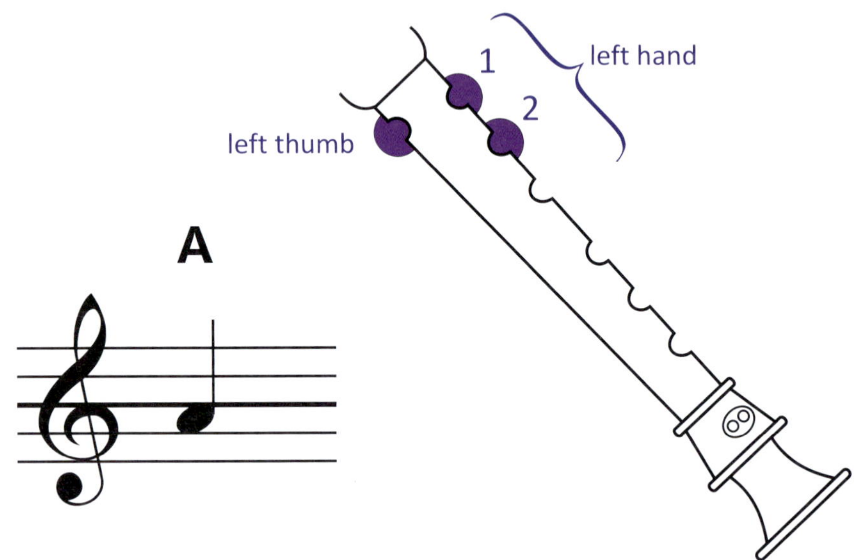

* Using the pads of the fingers ensures a good 'seal' and avoids squeaking.

Sing, Clap and Play 2

April

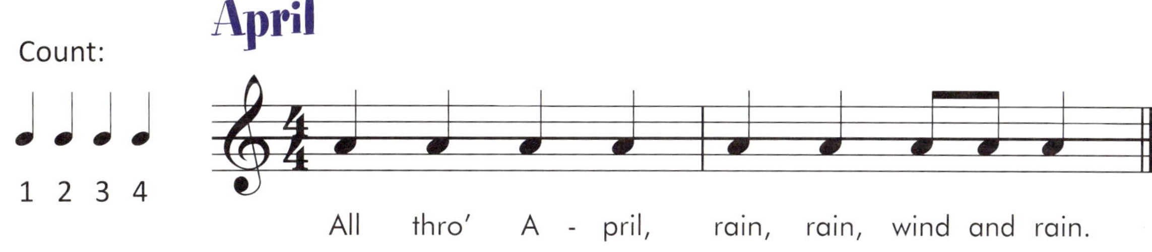

Acorns

Ants

Lesson 3

Hold your recorder, balancing the mouthpiece against your chin.

With your left thumb and first finger, make the note *B*.

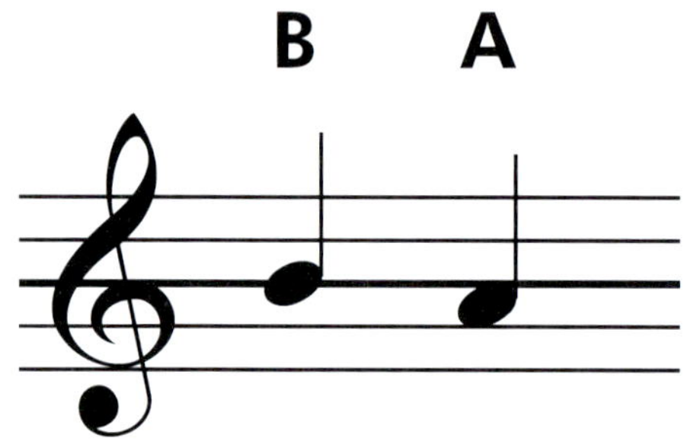

What must you do to make the note *A*?

That's right! It's simple. Just add your second finger and you are playing *A*.

Remove it, and you are back to *B*.

Try this several times with your recorder still on your chin. Then go on to the songs.

Don't forget to SING, CLAP and PLAY.

Sing, Clap and Play 3

At the beginning of every tune are two numbers.
These help to tell you the rhythm of the music.
Till now there have only been *walking* rhythms:

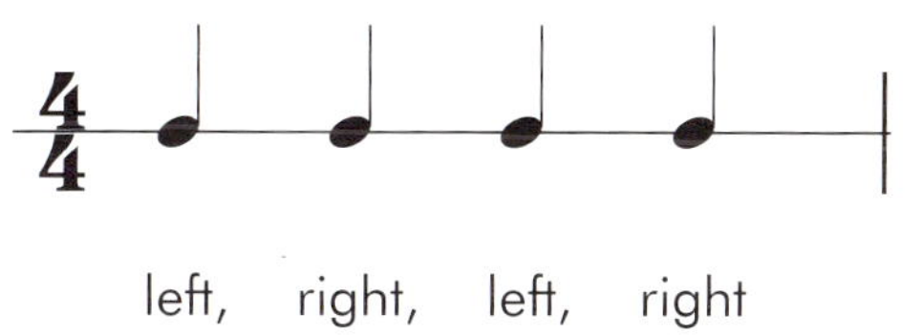

The new rhythm on this page is a **skipping** rhythm:

Skipping

Count:

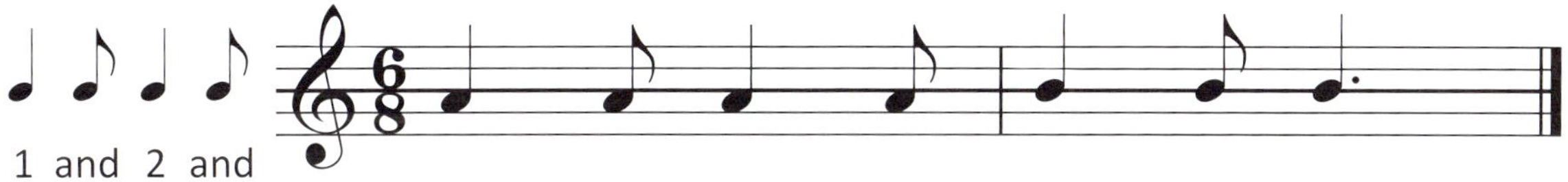

1 and 2 and

Humpty Dumpty

Count:

1 and 2 and

Jack

Count:

1 and 2 and

Lesson 4

Look at the picture on the right.

Can you see how to make the note *G*?

It is made with the thumb and three fingers of the left hand.

Keep practising *G* until you get a clear, round note.

If it squeaks, then you are not completely covering all the holes.*

Always listen to what you play.

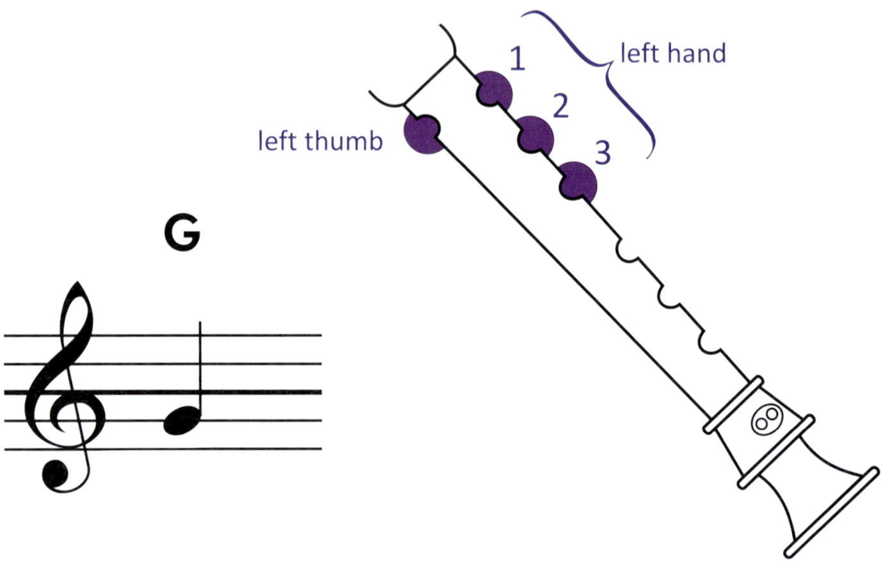

* Small hands often find it difficult to reach a *G*. Keeping the fingers at right angles to the recorder will make the task easier.

Sing, Clap and Play 4

Gilbert

Count:

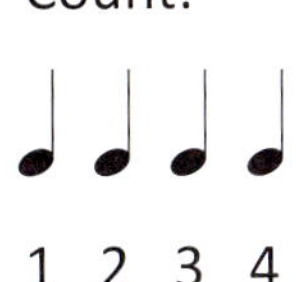

1 2 3 4

This sign  is called a rest.

It is placed where we want a gap
in the music instead of a note.

Gobble, gobble

Count:

1 2 3 4

Fly away

Count:

1 2 3 4

Lesson 5

So far you have learned the notes *B*, *A* and *G*.

With your recorder resting on your chin, make the note *G*.

Now lift your third finger.
What note are you playing?

Then lift your second finger.
What are you playing now?

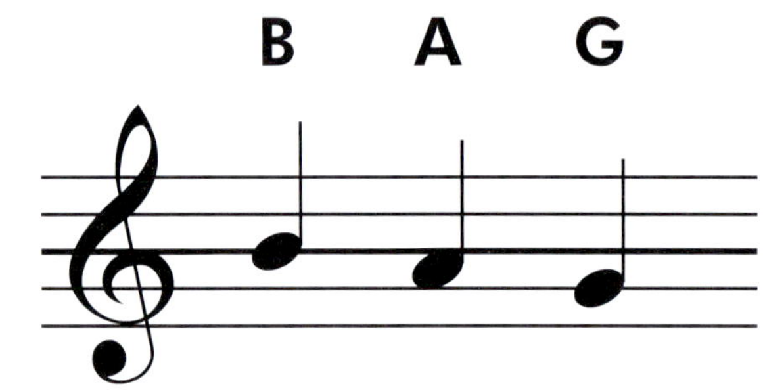

Keeping the recorder on your chin, practise this several times:

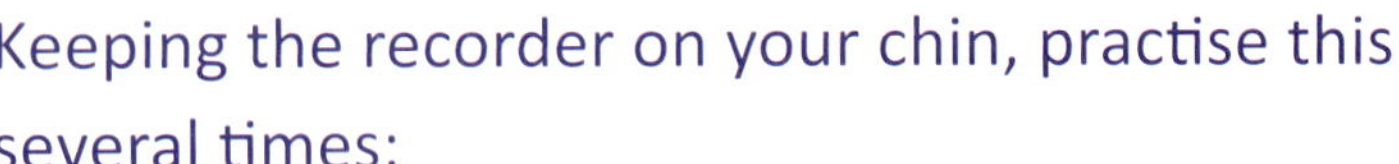

Now play it.

Sing, Clap and Play 5

This sign tells you to repeat the tune:

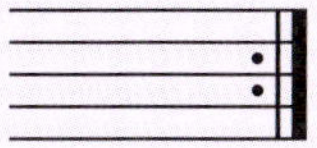

Fares please!

Count:

1 2 3 4

Goodnight

Count:

1 2 3 4

Chairs to mend

Count:

1 and 2 and

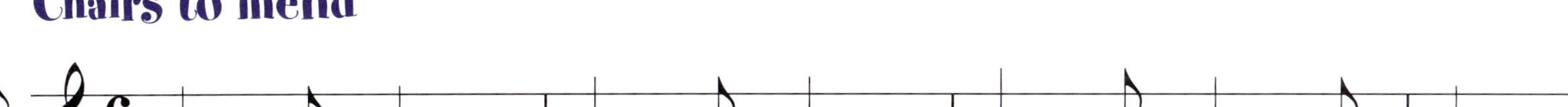

Lesson 6

Putting notes together can make a tune, but they don't always make good music.

Play this tune, tonguing every note:

(Doo - doo - doo - doo - doo - doo - doo.)

Now play the same tune again, tonguing every other note:

(Doo - oo   doo - oo   doo - oo   doo.)

Joining notes together like this:  is called *slurring*.

Another way of improving your music is to breathe in the right place.

This is a breathing mark: ✓

Sing, Clap and Play 6

Exercise 1

Count:

1 2 3 4

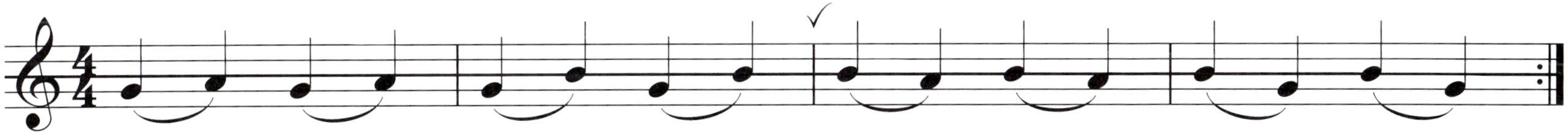

Exercise 2

Count:

1 2 3 4

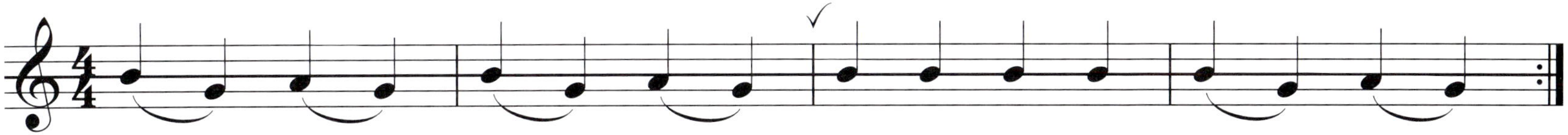

Goodnight

Count:

1 2 3 4

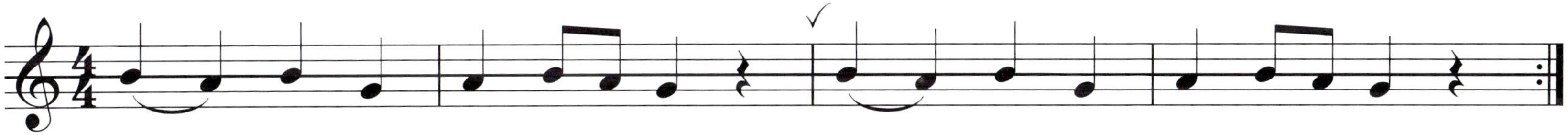

Concert 1

Au clair de la lune

Play it again!

Concert 1

Rowing

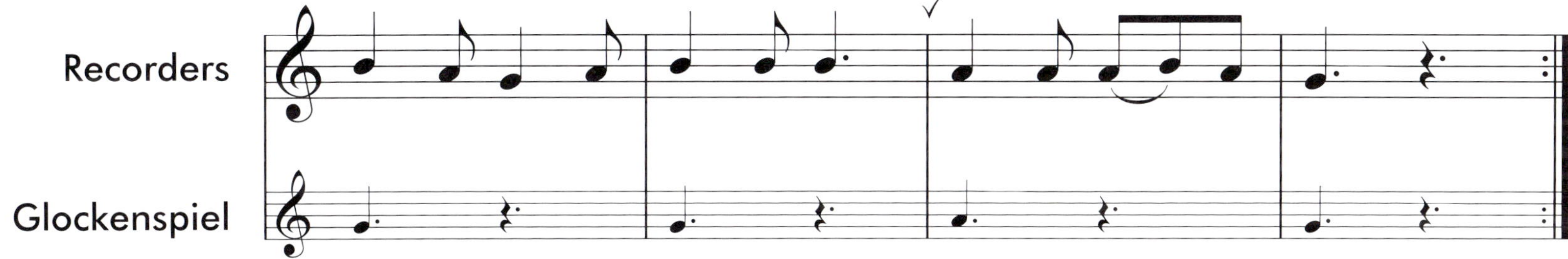

This tune has the same rhythm as 'Jack' on page 9,
but has a slower speed.

Concert 1

Chairs to mend

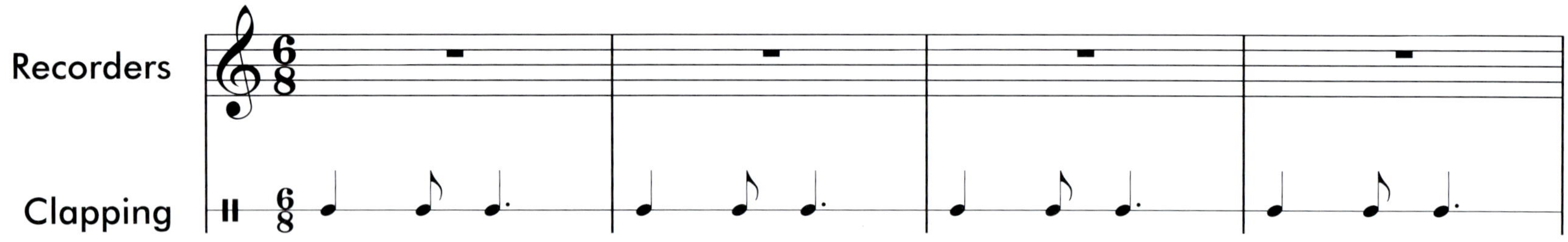

Concert 1

Frère Jacques

Lesson 7

With your recorder on your chin, make a *G*.

Now cover the next two holes with the first two fingers of your *right* hand.

This is the note *E*.

Lift them, and you're back to *G*.

Keep them close to the holes when you lift them off.

Practise changing from *G* to *E*, moving your two right-hand fingers on and off together.

Now play this:

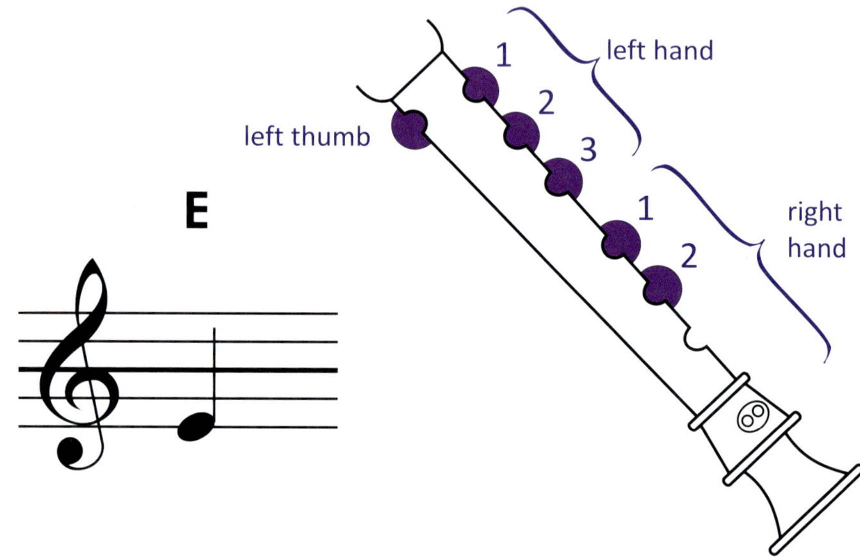

Sing, Clap and Play 7

On this page only half the words have been given. Can you write your own words to fit the rest of the rhythm?

All alone

Count:

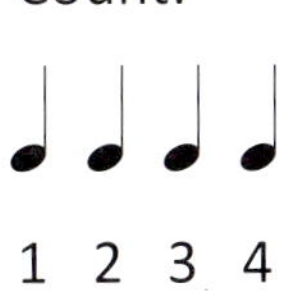

1 2 3 4

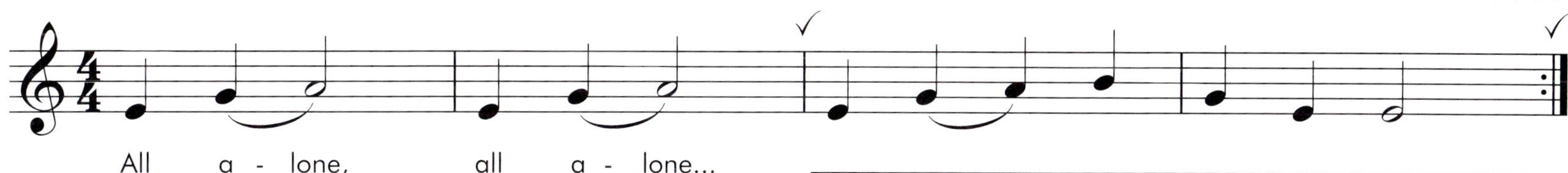

Cuckoo

Count:

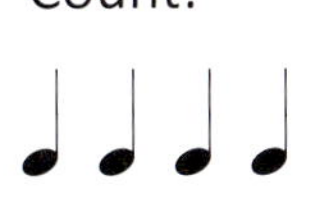

1 2 3 4

Girls and boys

Count:

1 and 2 and

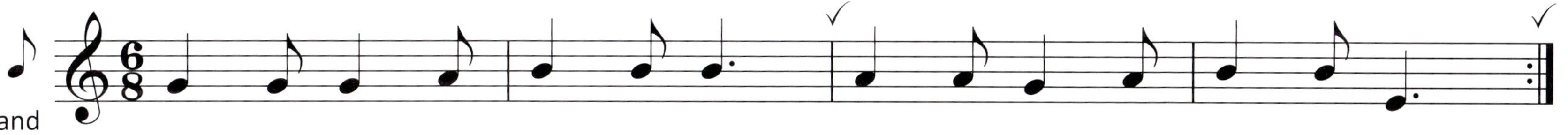

March of the soldiers

Count:

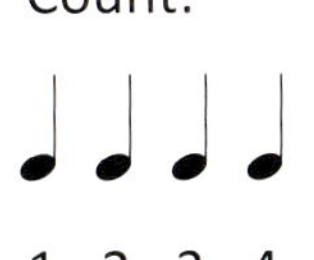

1 2 3 4

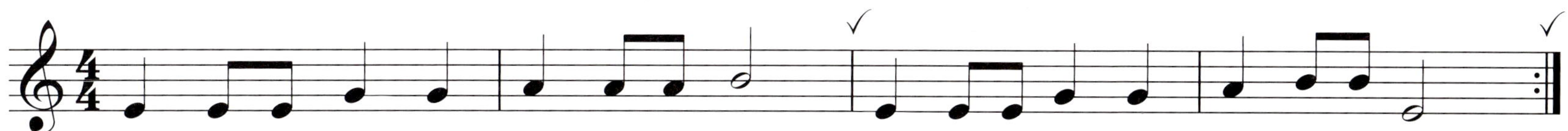

Lesson 8

Can you see from the diagram how to make the note *D*?

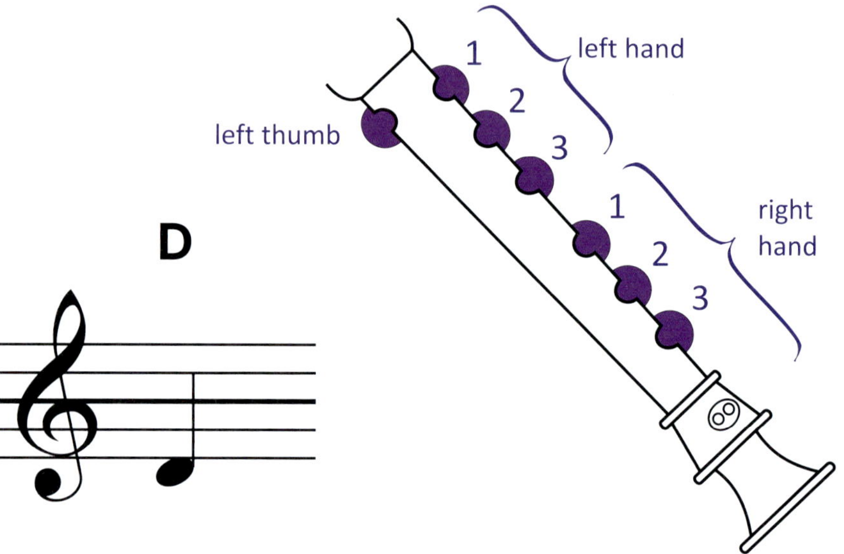

D

You use the thumb and three fingers of your *left* hand, and three fingers of your *right* hand.

Play a *D* and keep practising until you get a good, clear sound.

Then play this:

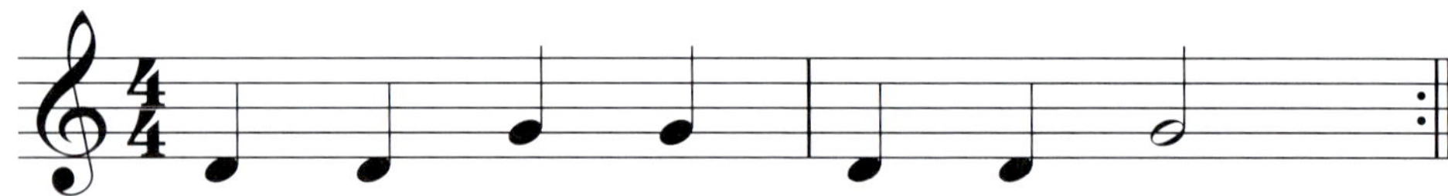

Sing, Clap and Play 8

Concert 2

Cuckoo

Concert 2

A march

Concert 2

Chinese bells

Concert 2

Skipping

All Recorders

Recorders 1

Recorders 2

In the second part of this tune, Recorders 1 start one bar before Recorders 2.

This is called a **round** or **canon**.

You can play this part several times.

Lesson 9

With your left thumb on the back hole, place your
second finger on the second hole.

This is the note *C*.

Blow it gently.

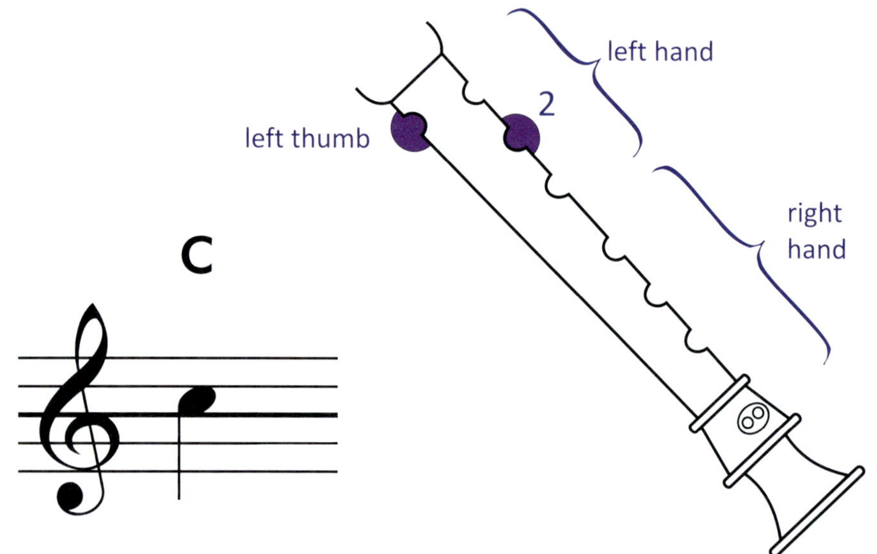

With your mouthpiece on your chin, practise
moving from C to A.

Now play this:

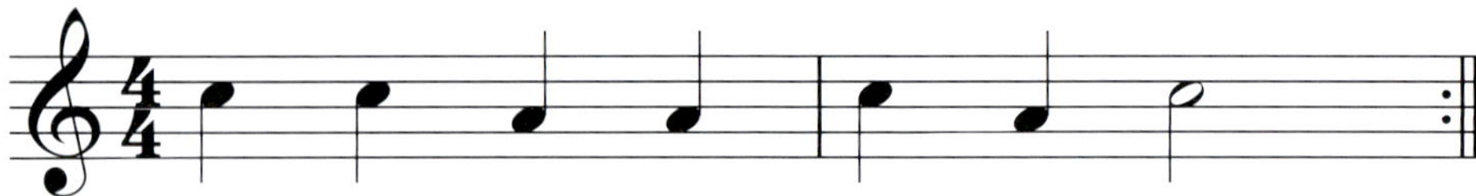

Next, practise moving from *C* to *B*.

Then play this, taking care to make each note smooth
and distinct.

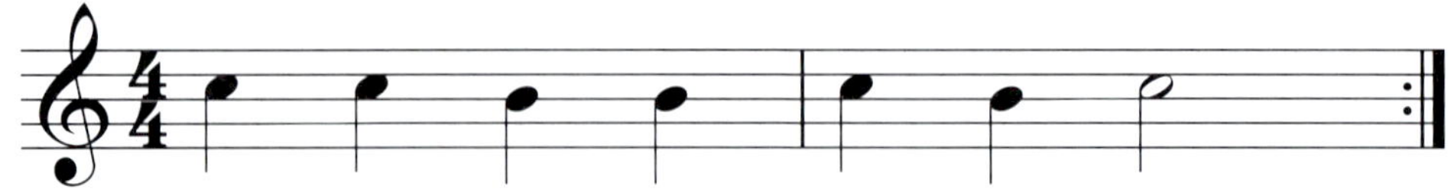

Sing, Clap and Play 9

Heave-ho!

Lesson 10

With your recorder on your chin, make the note *C*.

Lift off your *left* thumb and you're making a *D'*.

Practise this several times.

You will see how important it is to keep your right thumb in place!

Now play this exercise, blowing gently*.

D' (high D)

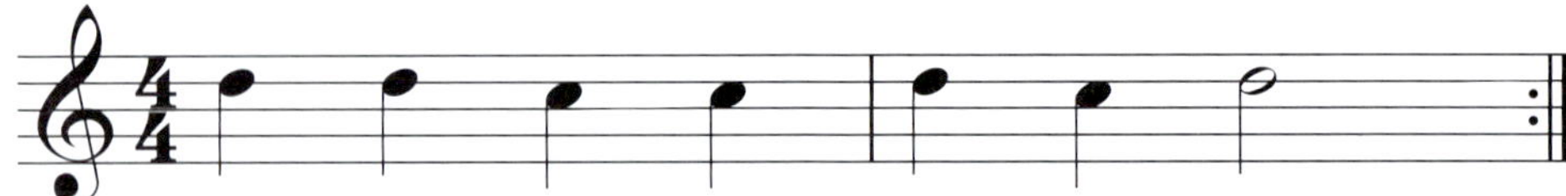

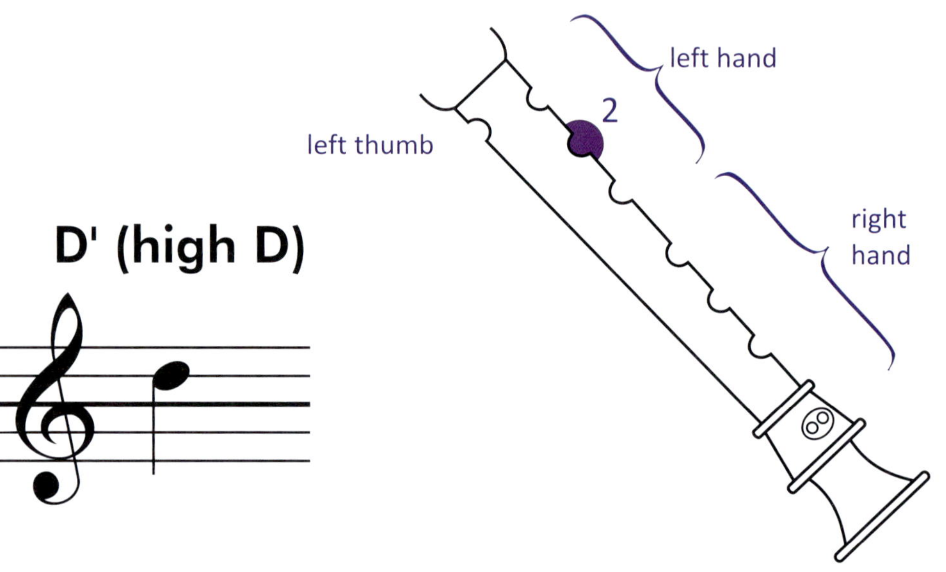

* Overblowing high notes is a common fault.

Sing, Clap and Play 10

When you have learnt these two Alpine songs, divide into two groups and play them together.

You will hear them fit with each other!

Lesson 11

This sign ♯ is called a **sharp**.

The new note we are learning is called **F sharp**, and is written **F♯**.

Play *F♯* and practise it several times*.

* It is important to check that each finger is on the correct hole, i.e. the first finger of the right hand is not used.

F♯ (sharp)

Sing, Clap and Play 11

March 1

Count:

March 2

When you have learnt these two marches, divide into two groups and play them together.

You will hear them fit with each other!

Concert 3

Sur le pont

Concert 3

Daisy, Daisy

Concert 3

March in G

Concert 3

Alpine song

Concert 3

Ode to joy Ludwig van Beethoven

Concert 3

Andante   Wolfgang Amadeus Mozart

Gently
Recorders
Glockenspiel
Recorders
Glockenspiel
Recorders
Glockenspiel
Recorders
Glockenspiel

This is to certify that

Name:

has completed Sing, Clap and Play book 1.

Teacher:

Date:

Heather Cox

Garth Rickard

The Latin 'Cantate, plaudite et ludite' means 'Sing, clap and play'.